FAMILY DIFFERENCES

HONOR HEAD

W

Franklin Watts
Published in paperback in Great Britain in 2019 by The Watts Publishing Group

Credits:
Series Editor: Jean Coppendale
Series Designer: Lorraine Inglis

Picture credits:
Every attempt has been made to clear copyright. Should there be any inadvertent omission please apply to the publisher for rectification.
t = top, b = bottom , l = left, r = right, m = middle
All images listed here are © of Shutterstock and: cover Marharyta Pavkiuk; title page Yulia Glam; 4-5 Zurijeta; 4bl x3 Marish, 5 talkback heads, DreamMaster; 6-7 background STILLFX, 6 Creative Mood; 8 emojis, flower travelin' man; 9bl Tinseltown; 10 Macrovector; 11 dramaiens; 12 pimchawee; 13 Lolostock; 14b Lorelyn Medina, 14t Stefan Holm; 15l Erik Lam; 16 wheelchair, Ellegant, 16t PiXXart; 18-19 background TashaNatasha,18 table, Nowik Sylwiaa, figure, majivecka; 19 Viktorija Reuta; 20 Lorelyn Medina; 22t zimmytws, 22b ostill; 23 Anna Violet; 24 retororcket; 25 puppies Erik Lam; 26-27 Bruce Rolff; 28-29 birds Mrs Opposum.

Note to parents and teachers: Every effort has been made by the Publishers to ensure that these websites are suitable for children, that they are of the highest educational value, and that they contain no inappropriate or offensive material. However, because of the nature of the Internet, it is impossible to guarantee that the contents of these sites will not be altered. We strongly advise that Internet access is supervised by a responsible adult.

ISBN 978 1 4451 5291 2

Printed in China

MIX
Paper from
responsible sources
FSC® C104740

Franklin Watts

An imprint of
Hachette Children's Group
Part of The Watts Publishing Group
Carmelite House
50 Victoria Embankment
London EC4Y 0DZ

An Hachette UK Company
www.hachette.co.uk

www.franklinwatts.co.uk

Contents

IDEA

#TRUST

FAMILIES TODAY

A typical family used to be mum, dad and two or three children but today there are many different types of family.

Not the same

Today's family could be same-sex parents, a single parent or a step- or blended family. You might live with foster parents, be adopted or be cared for by grandparents or other relatives. As more and more parents have to work longer hours, their children may be looked after by other family members even though they live at home. Some older children may look after their younger siblings or they may have the responsibility of caring for physically or mentally ill parents. There isn't such a thing as a 'typical' family.

Changes happen

Many children will experience changes to their family. Their parents may separate or divorce, a parent may die or, for whatever reason, a parent may decide that they can no longer look after their children. A new partner joining the family with their own children can make a huge impact, for good and for bad. More and more families do change and if this is happening to you, you are not alone.

Mixed families

Many families are now mixed race, and different religious beliefs can cause family tensions. Often second and third generations in immigrant families feel that the values of their parents and grandparents don't apply to them. They feel torn between their parents' beliefs and the values of the culture they have grown up with. It can be confusing for everyone.

TALKBACK!

Look out for the TALKBACK boxes. This is where you and your friends, family or classmates can discuss two sides of an argument. There are no right or wrong answers, but you might be surprised at the conclusions you come to.

FIGHTING FAMILIES

All families have their disagreements, and adults can get cross and lose their temper after a long day at work or if they're feeling stressed or tired. But sometimes things can take a turn for the worse ...

Under pressure

Some families have to face a lot of pressure every day. Maybe someone is out of work or ill, or they are working at two or three jobs to keep the family going. This can cause stress levels to rise, which can result in rows and arguments at home. Normally adults make up quickly and everything is forgotten, but if the rows become more frequent and more aggressive it can be very frightening if you have to witness it.

Domestic violence

Some adults, both men and women, can be violent towards their partners and children. This can happen for many reasons – stress, depression, drinking too much alcohol or taking drugs or because using violence makes some people feel powerful and in control. If your parents or carers fight, don't try and stop them or you might get hurt, just leave the room if you can. If you have younger siblings take them away from the fighting and try and keep them calm. If the fighting is violent and someone is being hurt, call the police or a nearby friend, family member or neighbour.

Let off steam

Some people often worry that if they come from a violent home, they will be violent themselves. This doesn't have to happen. If you always feel angry or have aggressive thoughts or want to punch and hit people, speak to a helpline, your doctor, or an adult you trust. Stress can make you feel angry and it will help to talk about it. Don't let your aggressive feelings get out of control. A great way to get rid of aggression safely is to join a sports group so you can let off steam in a controlled way. Try kickboxing, ring boxing, running or a martial art, such as karate. For more ideas on managing stress see page 13.

Feel safe

Lots of young people who live with domestic violence think that it's their fault the violence is happening or they don't report it in case they get their parents or carers into trouble. This anxiety can make you feel scared, stressed and guilty. It can cause sleeplessness or nightmares and can affect schoolwork. But domestic violence is never ever the child's fault, and if you feel in any danger you must tell someone.

If a friend is suffering from domestic violence, try and support them as much as possible. What they tell you they will probably want to keep confidential, so don't tell any of your other friends or put it out on social media.

7

LIVING APART

Couples decide to live apart for many reasons. If this happens it means huge changes for everyone in the family.

Divorce and separation

When couples decide to separate it could be because one partner has met someone else, or they have grown apart or they've fallen out of love with each other. Perhaps they were arguing a lot or felt they couldn't be happy together any more. Usually it is very sad for everyone, including the person leaving the family home. Most parents still love their children very much, even if they no longer want to live together.

Bad feelings

AFRAID

WORRIED

CONFUSED

GUILTY

HURT

ANGRY

SAD

Children can feel a range of emotions when their parents separate – guilt, thinking it was something they did or said to cause the break-up, fear about the future and sadness and anger at the change. They may feel they can't be friends with the parent who is leaving or they may hate both parents for breaking up. These are all normal feelings to have.

How to cope

At a time like this adults can be so involved with their own lives they may not realise the impact their behaviour is having on everyone else. Here are some ways to get through the difficult times.

- If you feel sad don't be embarrassed to tell someone and cry when you need to.
- If you feel angry try not to take it out on your siblings or school friends. It's easy to say and do hurtful things without meaning to when you feel hurt yourself.
- You don't have to take sides. Talk to both parents about your feelings.
- If one parent says bad things about the other one, tell them if it makes you angry or upset.
- If you find it difficult to talk to your parents, write them a letter or an email.

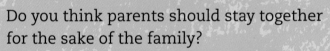

TALKBACK!

My parents' divorce left me with a lot of sadness ... and pain, and acting and especially humour, was my way of dealing with all that.

Jennifer Aniston (b. 1969), actress

Do you think parents should stay together for the sake of the family?

A bad atmosphere at home or parents shouting or being nasty to each other is worse than a divorce.

They are adults and should try and live together and get on for the sake of their family.

Single-parent family

Many children today are looked after by one parent only. Maybe parents have separated or one parent is not living at home for other reasons.

Just you!

Most single parents are mothers, but many are single fathers or even a single grandparent. Single parents may not work hours that fit in with school. This often means that the child has to make breakfast, get themselves ready for school and then to and from school, prepare a meal when they get home. Older children may have to look after younger siblings. If your parent works long hours and you spend a lot of time by yourself it can be lonely. Are there family members, or school friends, that you can stay with after school?

{ There's no need to be **embarrassed** or feel *ashamed* about your situation. }

Independent

Having to take care of yourself and perhaps a younger brother and sister can make you feel independent and grown-up. This can be good but you still need time to see your friends, chill out and do your homework. If you feel that you don't have the time or energy to do your schoolwork properly or feel you are missing out on seeing your friends or doing hobbies, have a chat with your parent about it. Maybe another member of the family could look after your siblings, or you could stay with a friend for a sleepover. Speak to your teacher if your schoolwork is suffering and explain what is happening so they can try to help.

New partner

If a parent meets a new partner this can cause mixed feelings. You may be pleased that your parent has met someone special but you might also feel jealous and feel that your space is being invaded by a stranger. Talk about it with your parent. Think about how good it is for your parent to have some support and fun with the new person. Join in and get to know the new family member. Maybe the new partner has children of their own who will become friends.

TRUST AND ABUSE

Your home should be a safe place and your family safe people to be with, but this isn't always the way it is.

Physical abuse

By law everyone has the right to be safe at home. Most families are caring and loving but not all families are the same. No adult has the right to hurt a child. If anyone in your family is physically hurting you, such as kicking, slapping, punching, pushing or beating you, you must report this to the police or tell a trusted adult. Sexual abuse is also against the law. If anyone is touching you in private places, making you feel embarrassed and forcing you to do things you don't want to, you must tell the police or a trusted adult or phone a helpline.

Emotional abuse

Abuse is not just about hurting someone physically. Being called names, being sworn and shouted at all the time or being ignored or made to feel stupid or inferior is emotionally damaging and a serious form of abuse. If you're not sure if what is happening to you is abuse, phone a helpline or speak to someone you trust about it. You shouldn't have to suffer any form of abuse from siblings, grandparents, parents, aunts, uncles or family friends.

Dark thoughts

Children abused at home can feel worthless, bad and out of control of their own lives. They might think stuff is happening because there is something wrong with them. Dark, negative feelings can build up inside and become uncontrollable. This can lead to the person hurting others or harming themselves as a way of coping with painful feelings, to punish themselves or to feel they have more control over their own life.

How to manage dark thoughts

★ Phone a helpline (see page 31). No one will judge you and all calls are treated with confidence. No one will make you do anything you don't want to.

★ If you don't feel ready to talk, join an online discussion forum and share your thoughts with others who might feel the same. Sometimes just knowing you're not the only one suffering these dark feelings can help.

★ Keep a journal. Write down what triggers the dark thoughts about yourself or others. It can really help to get them out in the open. If you're worried someone might find them, destroy them afterwards.

PROBLEMS WITH SIBLINGS

Our brothers and sisters can be our best friends for life, but there are no rules that say siblings have to get on, and many don't.

What a pest!

Most sibling arguments are part of growing up. An older sibling might be jealous because a younger one is getting more attention; a younger sibling might think the older one has more freedom. Siblings borrow from each other without asking, invade each other's space, can be embarrassing and generally a nuisance. This is all quite normal, but sometimes growing frustration and resentment becomes bullying, such as pushing, arm twisting, 'accidental' trips and falls, hurtful teasing and cyberbullying. If you're being bullied by a sibling tell an adult you trust. If you are the bully, talk to someone about your feelings and what is causing them.

Alistair: On the whole (our rivalry) was always positive. In the past there probably were times when we overstepped the line and fell out, but now it's always very productive.

Brothers Alistair (b. 1988) and Jonny (b. 1990) Brownlee, Olympic triathlon medal winners

Not my family!

Step- and half-siblings can be as close as biological siblings, but for some, living with half-siblings and step-siblings can be difficult. Maybe one child is given more or better presents or taken to smart places by their other parent. This can lead to jealousy, resentment and anger. These feelings can get out of hand and become an issue.

Try and have regular family get-togethers to discuss your feelings. If you feel angry and jealous all the time, or start to feel left out, unloved or second best, talk to your parents about it if you can. Your step-siblings are probably feeling angry and scared at the family changes as well, and your half-siblings are probably missing their other parent.

Only child

Some only children may wish they had brothers and sisters, while others are perfectly happy being the only child. As with all different family types, being an only child has its good points and its bad points. Only children often think there's a lot of pressure on them to do well at school. They may feel lonely and find it difficult to share their feelings. On the other hand, it can help them learn to be independent, they can spend time alone when they want to and they don't have to share their stuff!

TALKBACK!

Do you think brothers and sisters should try and be best friends?

I think it's important that brothers and sisters stick together no matter what happens.

As long as siblings are kind to each other they don't have to be best friends – after all, it's not like you choose your family as you do your friends.

CHILD CARERS

Young carers are children who look after a member of their family, such as a parent or younger brother or sister.

Hard work

Some children as young as 5 are carers, but the average age is about 8 to12. Young carers may look after a disabled or mentally ill parent or sibling. The caring they have to do can be very demanding and exhausting. They may have to get up early in the morning to get a parent up and washed, cook breakfast, give the parent their medication and make sure they are okay for the day, all before school. On the way home they may have to shop, then cook again in the evening and see their parent to bed.

'I miss a lot of school because I am tired. I often have to get up in the night to help my mum with her tablets.'

Rachel, 10 years

Missing out

Young carers do an amazing job but it can be stressful. If a child is supporting a parent with a drug or alcohol addiction they may feel too ashamed to talk about it. They don't want to betray their parent by sharing something private. They often miss out on school because the caring they do at home takes up a lot of time. They may not even have time to make friends. Young carers can have complex feelings to deal with – they might feel ashamed of a parent and angry with them and then guilty for having these feelings. They might feel anxious about the future, and be frustrated and resentful that their peers appear to be having a good time and they're not.

It's not fair!

Not alone

If you are a young carer you have rights and are entitled to help from social services who will send someone round to assess the situation and see what support they can give you. The social services are there to help you and won't judge you or your family or split you up unless it is really essential for everyone's well-being. There is no need to struggle alone. Contact organisations who have lots of support services and who will talk you through your options (see page 31). Talk to other family members and your teachers about the situation so they can give you additional practical and emotional support.

LIVING ON THE BREADLINE

Some families struggle to live on the money they have for many reasons, such as losing a job, not having enough work or giving up work to look after a sick partner or child.

Hide the facts

All types of families from any background can suddenly find themselves living on the breadline. This means they barely have enough money for essentials such as food, clothes and heating. Their homes may be damp and have mould that can make children ill. To feed their family parents may have to go to a food bank. Many parents and children feel ashamed if they have to live like this and hide it from friends and family. Parents juggling several different jobs to earn enough might not have the time or energy to care for their children properly.

Shame and loneliness

Young people from poor families are often hungry all the time, feel ashamed and anxious about the future and think that school is a waste of time. They don't have pocket money so cannot join in outings with friends and because they can't socialise with others they can become isolated and loners. It can be frustrating not to have the things that their peers have. For many young people having the latest trainers, smart phone or ipod is very important but possessions don't give us true happiness (although it may seem like it at the time).

Just because your classmates have their own room, **pocket money** and the latest clothes, doesn't mean they are any *better* or any **happier** than you.

Take control

Living on the breadline can seem hopeless but there are things you can do. Phone a helpline or speak to a trusted adult about finding practical help. Ask at school about free breakfast or after-school clubs. If you have a local library this is a warm and quiet place to do homework. Don't be bullied into feeling ashamed or less worthy than your peers. Believe in yourself and stay positive. You can have as bright a future as anyone else. You might need to work a little harder for it but this will make you a stronger person.

MY LIFE!

Pre-teen and teenage years are a challenging time when children are becoming young adults and begin to question their parents' values and beliefs.

It's my life!

Pre-teen or teenage years are when you start to want to develop a life outside of the family, with your own friends, school commitments, hobbies, goals and ideas about yourself and your future. Friends and peers become really important and the need to be part of a group or crowd is very strong. Family expectations can begin to seem like they're stopping you from living your life.

Culture clash

Following your own dreams can be more difficult for second and third generations of migrant families who might be trying to please their parents at home and fit in with their peers at school. They may feel they belong to both cultures and don't want to 'betray' either one. Trying to manage both sets of values can cause tension and arguments at home. Share your feelings with your parents and see if you can come to a compromise. Sadly, some beliefs can be a threat to young people. If family members are planning anything that will harm you or is against the law, such as a forced marriage or FGM, call a helpline, tell a teacher or go to the police.

Parents' responsibility

Until you are 18 years old your parents have a legal responsibility to care for you. If you live at home this means you have to live by the house rules and do as your parents ask. Although the rules may seem like a punishment, they are usually for your own good. If you feel that your parents are being unreasonable or over-strict, try not to get angry, shout or leave the room slamming the door behind you. Explain your feelings, listen to their concerns and be prepared to compromise.

TALKBACK!

Parents can be a huge problem for young people. What do you think is the best way to tackle them?

Tell them that you are old enough to lead your life the way you want to. If they care about you they'll let you do what you want.

Try and understand that because they care about you they are only doing what they think is best for you, even if you don't agree!

FAMILY BREAK DOWN

Sometimes situations at home are so serious that the family has to be broken up. This is never an easy time for anyone.

Staying together

Generally children and young people would rather try and cope with any problems at home themselves than speak to someone in authority outside the family about what is happening. The thought of the family being broken up can stop a lot of young people reporting abuse or violence or difficult situations at home.

Keep safe

Parents or other family members may try and persuade you not to tell anyone about bad things happening at home. They may try to make you feel guilty or ashamed or scared of what might happen if you do. But living in a home that is violent or abusive can cause long-lasting damage to your mental and emotional well-being. You have to do what will keep you and your brothers and sisters safe. If you have any doubt about what to do, call a helpline and they will advise you, but they won't do anything you don't want them to.

Crisis!

Problems such as stress, poverty and debt, anxiety, fear, exhaustion, isolation and abuse can sometimes lead a parent to have a mental breakdown. As a result of mental illness or addiction some parents decide that they are no longer able to look after their children. If the family is in crisis, drastic changes might need to happen to keep the children safe. Whatever the reason, if a child is being neglected (not fed, clothed or looked after properly), abused or harmed in any way, the social services might decide to take them away from the family for their own safety. This will only happen as a last resort.

Safe refuge

Women and children who are threatened with domestic violence might be sent to a refuge. A refuge centre is a house where families can stay where they will be safe from the violence at home. The family will usually have their own bedrooms and share a kitchen and bathroom. The people who run the refuge centre will help you to settle in and give advice and support. Once it is safe, the family usually goes back home.

Children taken away from the **family home** might be placed with a relative, put into foster care or, in extreme cases, put up for *adoption*.

Foster care and adoption

If a family is having a major crisis the children might
be put into foster care or adopted for their own safety.

What is foster care?

Foster care or fostering is when a child stays with a
family that will look after the child until it is safe for the
child to go home, or until a more permanent home is found.
Fostering can be for a few days, weeks, months
or several years. Foster families can give the
child the safety and security that is missing
at home, but fostering is not permanent.
If circumstances improve, the child may
be able to go back to their own family.

A **foster family**
is often a
lifeline
when a child can't
stay at home.

What is adoption?

Adoption is permanent. When a family adopts a child they take on all the legal responsibilities for that child as if the child were their own. Children can be adopted at any age from babies to pre-teens. Step-parents often adopt their step-children, which means they then take over all legal rights from the biological parents.

If you are adopted by a step-parent you may feel that you have to choose between them and your real parent and feel angry, sad and confused. Talk to your family about how you feel, call a helpline or speak to a friend or trusted adult. Don't bottle up your feelings or get angry with your new family. They only want the best for you.

Your new home

Foster and adopted children have every right to be loved and cared for as much as anyone else. Foster homes are safe and secure places where you will be well looked after. Some foster homes may have more than one foster child staying, others may have their own children. It can be difficult to settle into a new home and make friends with the other children.

Be polite and courteous and follow the house rules, but talk to your foster parents and social worker if you have any worries or concerns or if you miss your family. If you experience bullying or mental or physical abuse in a foster home or with adopted parents, you should report it to a social worker or an adult you trust or go to the police.

Illness and death

When a parent, carer, grandparent, sibling or other close family member becomes very ill or dies it can be devastating for the family.

Traumatic time

It is traumatic for children to witness parents or siblings with an illness such as cancer or to watch a loved grandparent struggle with dementia or a stroke. Watching someone you love suffer can make you feel anxious, sad, angry and scared. If it is a sibling you may feel guilty that you are so fit and healthy and feel bad about enjoying yourself.

Who's special?

A child with a sibling who has an illness or special needs might start to feel jealous and resentful towards that sibling, especially if they seem to be getting all of their parents' attention. This is normal and there is no need to feel ashamed or embarrassed, but try and talk to someone about your feelings. Parents might be so concerned about the sick sibling that they don't realise how the whole situation is affecting you. This doesn't mean they love you any less. Offer to help with your brother or sister but remember that it's not your responsibility to look after your siblings.

Not alone

Losing someone close to you can shake your whole world. It could make you feel scared, lonely, isolated, angry, withdrawn and sad, or you might feel that you're going crazy – you want to cry all the time, forget things, can't concentrate at school and can't sleep. This is all part of grieving. For young people it can be an especially tough time as they are often the only student in their school who has experienced a loss. Schoolmates may not know how to react and may try and avoid them, making them feel even more isolated. Adults can feel uncomfortable talking about death or don't know what to say, especially if they are suffering, too.

Good to talk

Talking to someone can really help you to come to terms with a death. It is important that you express your anger and any fears and anxieties about what has happened. Talk to a teacher or relative if you can, or check out an online support site, such as the Childhood Bereavement Network (see page 31). Writing things down might also help you to understand your feelings.

TALKBACK!

If someone in your class lost a family member, how would you react?

Give them space to get over it. I wouldn't know what to say anyway.

I think you just need to act like you always do. They need to know they have a friend who's there for them.

SO, TO RECAP...

This is a recap of some of the issues in this book presented as ideas to discuss. Talking things through can help us to understand how we react to situations and to get an idea of how other people feel. A great way to deal with family issues is to spend time together as a family. Go for a walk together, watch a film or just chat over a pizza.

Stay Safe

All children have the right to be safe and secure at home, and most are. But some families may have fights or bully and abuse each other. Why do you think this might happen? Is there ever an acceptable reason for violent behaviour? What is the best way to stay safe if there is violence at home?

Breaking up

Parents divorcing or separating these days is very common and happens for many reasons. How do you think a divorce or separation affects the children? Is it fair that children are sometimes caught in the middle of parents who are separating? How can parents make sure this doesn't happen?

Total trust

Home should be a place where we feel safe and secure and where we are looked after and cared for. Families should trust each other and look out for one another. What kind of behaviour do you think is unacceptable from a family? What are the best ways to tackle abuse in a family?

Who needs siblings?

Our brothers and sisters can be friends for life and can be there to support us and help see us through good times and bad. Do you think siblings should always get on? Why would they not get on? Do you think a relationship with step-siblings could ever be the same as one with biological brothers or sisters?

Feeling ashamed

Some young people might spend a lot of their time feeling ashamed or embarrassed by their family circumstances. Their family might need to go to a food bank, or they have to look after a sick parent at home. Is it fair or right that young people feel ashamed in these circumstances?

Glossary

adopted when a child is legally looked after by people that are not their biological family

biological siblings brothers and sisters that have one or both birth parents in common

blended family a family consisting of children the parents have had and children from previous relationships

breadline on the breadline means struggling to cope financially

compromise when two or more people reach an agreement by giving up something they wanted

cultures the beliefs and behaviour of different places and people

depressed feeling sad and negative and with no energy or enthusiasm for anything

expectations what people want you to achieve

food bank a place where people go to get free food because they cannot afford to buy enough to feed their family

foster home another way to describe a foster family or foster parents

foster parents people who look after a child full time on a temporary basis

grieving a feeling of loss; feeling sad and missing the person who has died

inadequate not good enough

independent being able to care for yourself and make your own decisions

inferior not as good as someone or something else

immigrant a person who moves to another country to live there permanently

isolated alone; feeling like an outsider or different from other people

migrant a person who has moved to another country

mixed race people from two different countries

peers your friends or classmates; people of your own age

rivalry competition, trying to do something better than another person

siblings brothers and sisters

social services professional services funded by the government to help people who are going through difficult times

step-family when one parent and siblings are from another marriage or relationship

stress tension and worry especially if you feel you can't do what is expected or it is very difficult

values the beliefs and ways of living that people feel are important

Learning new words helps you to express your feelings and to understand what you read in this book.

Further information

Note to parents and teachers: every effort has been made by the publishers to ensure that; websites are suitable for children, that they are of the highest educational value, and that they contain no inappropriate or offensive material. However, because of the nature of the Internet, it is impossible to guarantee that the contents of these sites will not be altered. We strongly advise that Internet access is supervised by a responsible adult.

WEBSITES AND HELPLINES

If you feel overwhelmed by any of the issues you've read about in this book or need advice, check out a website or call a helpline and talk to someone who will understand.

www.childline.org.uk

Find out about issues that are troubling you, meet others, message or call the 24-hour helpline for advice or someone who'll just listen.
Telephone: 0800 1111

www.childhoodbereavementnetwork.org.uk
http://childbereavementuk.org/young-people/

Sites that will support for you while grieving.

www.hopeagain.org.uk

A support network for grieving young people. They have a free helpline 0808 808 1677 Monday–Friday, 9:30 am–5:00 pm.

https://karmanirvana.org.uk/

Phone in confidence if you are being forced into a marriage or suffering from honour-based abuse. Telephone: 0800 5999 247

www.themix.org.uk

A free online counselling and support service for people under 25 covering all issues, from self-harm to work problems. Telephone: 0808 808 4994

www.macmillan.org.uk/information-and-support/organising/practical-preparation-for-treatment/young-carers

Support and guidance for young carers aged under 18.

www.nhs.uk/conditions/social-care-and-support-guide/support-and-benefits-for-carers/being-a-young-carer-your-rights/

Guidance and advice on the rights of young carers.

www.barnardos.org.uk/

A place where children and young people can go for advice and support on topics such as poverty, bereavement, bullying, caring, fostering and other family issues.

www.sane.org.uk/

Online and phone help for mental and emotional issues with a dedicated helpline for young people.

For readers in Australia and New Zealand

https://youngcarersnetwork.com.au/

An online organisation helping young carers cope.

https://kidshelpline.com.au

Online and phone help for a wide range of issues.

www.cyh.com

Loads of online info about all sorts of issues including family stuff such as being an only child, being the eldest and being the youngest.

www.kidsline.org.nz

Helpline run by specially trained young volunteers to help kids and teens deal with troubling issues and problems.

BOOKS

What in the World Do You Do When Your Parents Divorce?: A Survival Guide for Kids by Kent Winchester & Roberta Beyer, Free Spirit Publishing 2002

Index